M000119592

This book belongs to

_____

MY VERY FIRST
BOOK of

BIBLE
FUN FACTS

The Bible version used in this publication is *The New King James Version.* Copyright © 1979, 1980, 1982, Thomas Nelson, Inc.

My Very First Book of Bible Fun Facts
ISBN 1-56292-682-9

Text copyright © 1994, 2001 by Mary Hollingsworth

Copyright © 1994, 2001 by Educational Publishing Concepts, Inc.
P.O. Box 665
Wheaton, Illinois 60189

Published by Honor Kidz
An Imprint of Honor Books, Inc.
P.O. Box 55388
Tulsa, Oklahoma 74155

Printed in China. All rights reserved under International Copyright Law. Contents and/or cover may not be reproduced in whole or in part in any form without the express written consent of the Publisher.

MY VERY FIRST
BOOK OF

BIBLE
FUN FACTS

Mary Hollingsworth

Illustrated by
Rick Incrocci

HONOR
kidz

An Imprint of Honor Books, Inc.
Tulsa, Oklahoma

Dear Parents,

Some people think that learning facts is boring. That may be true of ordinary facts, but that is not true of the extraordinary facts in the Bible.
Only God is capable of doing the miraculous and superhuman acts recorded in the Bible as facts. And children will delight in learning the exciting truths about God and His servants.

This book provides your child with important facts that will build faith and admiration for God. Your child will come away from the experience of this book with a thrill of learning about God and His mighty works.

We have focused the book on the incredible facts of the Bible, and we have included some activities just for fun to help the child remember those facts forever. Who knows, you may even learn some exciting facts yourself. Enjoy!

Mary Hollingsworth

It's a Fact

The word *Bible* means "books."

Your Bible is God's library. It has 66 different books in it! The Old Testament has 39 books. The New Testament has 27 books.

Just for Fun

Pretend that you are at God's library. Choose only one of the books in the Bible library to read. You might like the exciting book of Jonah that tells about Jonah being swallowed by a giant fish.

It's a Fact

God made the whole world and everything in it!

He made the land, seas, and sky. He made the animals, fish, and birds. He made the plants and trees. He even made you and me!

Just for Fun

Using some modeling clay, make a round ball that looks like the world. Put your world on a piece of paper and make animals, people, and plants to place around it.

In the beginning God created the
heavens and the earth.

Genesis 1:1

It's a Fact

Noah built a boat that was larger than a football field!

God told Noah to build a huge boat called an ark. The ark was about 450 feet long. That is bigger than a whole football field. No wonder Noah could put so many animals on the boat.

Just for Fun

The next time you go by a football field in your town, ask if you may stop to see how big Noah's ark was.

God said, "Build a boat for yourself. . . .
Make it 450 feet long, 75 feet wide, and
45 feet high."

Genesis 6:14-15 TEV

It's a Fact

God made a promise with a rainbow!

God put a beautiful rainbow in the sky after the Flood. It was God's sign that He would never again destroy the world with a flood.

Just for Fun

The rainbow always has seven pretty colors in it. They are red, orange, yellow, green, blue, indigo, and violet. With your crayons, draw God's wonderful rainbow, using the same colors He used.

The rainbow shall be seen in the cloud; and I will remember My [promise] . . . the waters shall never again become a flood to destroy all [the world].

Genesis 9:14-15

It's a Fact

A person once wrestled all night long!

One night a Man and Jacob had a wrestling match. The Man said, "Let Me go because it is almost morning." But Jacob said, "Not unless You bless me!" He said to Jacob, "You have struggled with God and with men, and have prevailed. . . . And He blessed him." God had blessed Jacob.

Just for Fun

Ask an adult to play wrestle with you.

Jacob was left alone; and a Man
wrestled with him.

Genesis 32:24

It's a Fact

A slave boy once ended up in a palace!

Young Joseph was a slave in Egypt. He had to do whatever he was told. Joseph pleased the king. The king trusted Joseph. The king made Joseph a leader.

Just for Fun

Using paper and crayons, draw a picture of a king.

Pharaoh said to Joseph, "You shall be over my house, and all my people shall be ruled according to your word."

Genesis 41:40

It's a Fact

An angel once appeared in a burning bush!

One day Moses was out in the field taking care of the sheep. He saw a bush that was on fire. An angel talked to Moses from inside the burning bush! The bush kept burning, but it never burned up.

Just for Fun

With your art scissors, cut out the shape of a fire from a piece of red paper. Then draw an angel on the fire.

And the Angel of the Lord appeared to him in a flame of fire from the midst of a bush.

Exodus 3:2

It's a Fact

God once turned a stick into a snake!

Moses and Aaron tried to get Pharaoh to free their people. To show Pharaoh how powerful God was, Aaron threw his rod (a wooden stick) on the ground. God turned it into a snake!

Just for Fun

Pretend you are a snake. Wiggle around on the floor.

Aaron cast down his rod before Pharaoh and before his servants, and it became a [snake].

Exodus 7:10

It's a Fact

God once parted the Red Sea!

God's people were trapped between the Red Sea and enemy soldiers. God saved them by pushing back the waters and making a dry path right through the sea. The people walked through the sea to safety.

Just for Fun

Using paper and crayons, draw a picture of the Israelites walking through the Red Sea.

So the children of Israel went into the
midst of the sea on the dry ground.

Exodus 14:22

It's a Fact

God made food appear in the desert every day for forty years!

God took care of His people. He sent them bread from heaven to eat. They found it on the ground each morning. The people did not know what the bread was, so they called it *manna*. *Manna* means "What is it?"

Just for Fun

Manna tasted like bread made with honey. Ask someone to put some honey on a piece of bread for you. Pretend that it is manna and eat it as God's people did.

They said to one another, "What is it?"
... Moses said to them, "This is the bread
which the LORD has given you to eat."

Exodus 16:15

It's a Fact

God filled a tent with His Holy Spirit!

Did you know that God once sent His Spirit to a tent? It was a holy tent called the tabernacle. God's tent was in the middle of His people's camp. He wanted to be close to the people He loved so much.

Just for Fun

Make a play tent in your yard or in your room with some old blankets or quilts. Sit in your tent and say a prayer to God. Thank Him for loving you.

And the glory of the Lord filled the tabernacle.

Exodus 40:34

It's a Fact

God once made a donkey talk!

One day, Balaam's donkey stopped when it saw God's angel blocking their path. Balaam hit the donkey to make it go on. Then the donkey started talking. It said, "Why are you hitting me?"

Just for Fun

Ask an adult to read you the story of Balaam in Numbers 22:21-35.

Then the LORD opened the mouth of the donkey, and she [spoke] to Balaam.

Numbers 22:28

It's a Fact

There are giants in the Bible!

The biggest giant in the Bible was a man named Og. He was the king of Bashan. The Bible says Og's bed was over thirteen feet long.

Just for Fun

Measure how long your own bed is. How much longer was Og's bed than yours?
Name another giant mentioned in the Bible.

King Og was the last of the [giants]. His coffin . . . was six feet wide and almost fourteen feet long.

Deuteronomy 3:11 TEV

It's a Fact

Spies escaped from their enemies by sliding down a rope!

In Bible times people made thread from a plant called flax. The thread was made into clothes and ropes. The rope Rahab used to help Joshua's spies escape down the city wall in Jericho may have been made of flax.

Just for Fun

Using some cotton twine, try to braid a small rope. If you need some help, ask an adult to show you how.

Then [Rahab] let them down by a rope
through the window, for her house was
on the city wall.

Joshua 2:15

It's a Fact

God made the wall of a city fall down!

Toot! Toot! Do you have a horn you can blow? Trumpets in the Bible were made of horns from male sheep. When God's priests blew horns at Jericho, God made the city wall fall down.

Just for Fun

March around your room seven times, and then blow a toy horn as the priests did at Jericho.

So the people shouted when the priests blew the trumpets. And . . . the wall fell down flat.

Joshua 6:20

It's a Fact

The sun once stood still!

God made the sun stop moving across the sky. Then His people had more daylight to win a battle against their enemies.

Just for Fun

Set up a battle between your toy soldiers or dolls. Pretend that one set is God's people. The other set is the enemy. Hold a flashlight over the armies like the sun. Let God's people win as long as the flashlight is on.

So the sun stood still, and the moon stopped, till the people had revenge upon their enemies.

Joshua 10:13

It's a Fact

Music made a king feel better!

David played his harp for King Saul. His music made King Saul feel happy. David's harp was probably a *lyre*. A lyre was a small harp that David could hold in his lap to play. He could carry it with him when he traveled.

Just for Fun

If you have a musical instrument, play a happy song or sing to someone in your family.

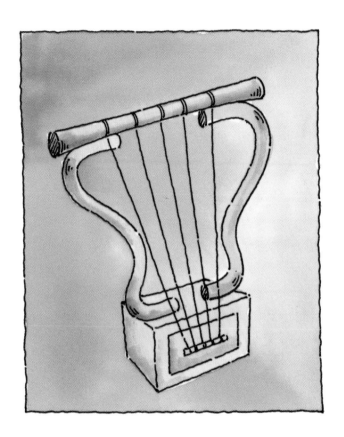

David would take a harp and play it with his hand. Then Saul would become refreshed and well.

1 Samuel 16:23

It's a Fact

A child fought a giant and won!

David slung a stone and knocked a giant down. The stone David used probably weighed about two pounds. And the sling was a real soldier's weapon. It was no wonder Goliath fell down!

Just for Fun

With some paper and crayons, draw a picture of David and Goliath. Make Goliath very big!

Then David . . . slung [the stone] and
struck the Philistine in his forehead.

1 Samuel 17:49

It's a Fact

A big, black bird once fed a man!

Elijah was hiding from his enemies. He was hiding in a cave by a stream. God had told him to go there. Every day God sent big, black ravens to bring food to Elijah.

Just for Fun

Take some bread crumbs outside. Throw them on the ground and watch quietly as birds come to eat them.

The ravens brought him bread and meat
in the morning, and bread and meat in
the evening.

1 Kings 17:6

It's a Fact

God sent fire from the sky!

The prophets of Baal asked him to send fire to their altar. Baal did not do it. Elijah asked God to send fire. God did! Fire came from the sky and burned the altar and the water around it!

Just for Fun

Using paper and crayons, draw a picture of the fire.

Then the fire of the LORD fell and . . . it
licked up the water that was in the
trench.

1 Kings 18:38

It's a Fact

A man rode in a whirlwind to get to heaven!

God loved Elijah so much that Elijah did not have to die. Elijah and his friend Elisha were walking down the road one day. Swish! A big whirlwind came down. Elijah left Elisha and rode the whirlwind right into heaven!

Just for Fun

Ask an adult to show you the picture of a whirlwind (tornado) in the dictionary or encyclopedia.

And Elijah went up by a whirlwind into heaven.

2 Kings 2:11

It's a Fact

A dead boy lived twice!

A little boy died. His mother was very sad. God's prophet Elisha prayed for God to make the boy alive again. He did!

Just for Fun

Say a prayer to God thanking Him for your life and for your family.

Then the child sneezed seven times, and the child opened his eyes.

2 Kings 4:35

It's a Fact

An eight-year-old child became king!

A young boy who was only eight years old once became king! Josiah was a good king who did what was right. God let him be king for thirty-one years.

Just for Fun

Pretend that you are king or queen of God's people. What kind of laws would you make for the people to follow?

Josiah was eight years old when he became king, and he reigned thirty-one years in Jerusalem.

2 Kings 22:1

It's a Fact

A king wanted everyone to worship him!

The king of Babylon made a golden statue. It was a huge statue of himself. It was ninety feet tall and nine feet wide! He told all the people to bow down and worship the statue.

Just for Fun

Using your art scissors and some gold-colored paper, cut out the shape of a statue. Then draw a face of a false god on the statue.

King Nebuchadnezzar had a gold statue made, ninety feet high and nine feet wide.

Daniel 3:1 TEV

It's a Fact

Three of God's people once walked in a fiery furnace and were not hurt!

Shadrach, Meshach, and Abed-Nego would not bow down to a false god. The king of Babylon put them in a fiery furnace. They were not hurt. God saved them! Then the king believed in God and took down his statue.

Just for Fun

Tear up the paper statue you made of the false god in the last lesson. Say, "There is only one real God."

The hair of their head was not [burned]
nor were their garments affected, and the
smell of fire was not on them.

Daniel 3:27

It's a Fact

God kept hungry lions from hurting a man!

God's servant Daniel was put into a den of lions to be killed. But God closed the lions' mouths, and they did not hurt Daniel.

Just for Fun

Ask an adult to take you to the zoo so that you can see the lions and listen to them roar.

Daniel said, "My God sent His angel and shut the lions' mouths, so that they have not hurt me."

Daniel 6:22

It's a Fact

A person lived inside a fish for three days!

God sent Jonah to preach to the evil city of Nineveh. Jonah did not want to go to Nineveh. So, he ran away from God and was swallowed by a giant fish. When God saved him from the fish, Jonah went to Nineveh.

Just for Fun

Ask an adult to take you to a fish store or an aquarium. What is the biggest fish you have ever seen?

And Jonah was in the belly of the fish three days and three nights.

Jonah 1:17

It's a Fact

A single star led wise men to the baby Jesus.

On the night that Jesus was born, a bright star was seen in the sky. Wise men in the East saw the star. They knew it was Jesus' star. So, they followed the star to see young Jesus.

Just for Fun

Have an adult help you use a telescope or a pair of binoculars. Look for the beautiful Eastern Star in the night sky.

The wise men said, "We have seen
[Jesus'] star in the East and have come
to worship Him."

Matthew 2:2

It's a Fact

Wise men brought gifts to a child!

The wise men brought gifts when they came to see Jesus. They brought gold, frankincense and myrrh.

Just for Fun

Ask someone to let you smell the vanilla you probably have in your kitchen. Notice that it smells sweet like myrrh.

And when they had opened their
treasures, they presented gifts to Him:
gold, frankincense, and myrrh.

Matthew 2:11

It's a Fact

The word *gospel* means "good news."

In the New Testament, there are four books that are called gospels. Matthew, Mark, Luke, and John tell the good news about Jesus Christ. He is the Son of God!

Just for Fun

Make a good news greeting card for someone you love. On the inside write, "Jesus loves you, and so do I." Ask an adult to help you mail the card.

And Jesus went about all Galilee, . . .
preaching the gospel of the kingdom.
Matthew 4:23

It's a Fact

More than five thousand people were
fed with one lunch!

Jesus was preaching. The people were
hungry. A little boy had five small
loaves of bread and two fish. Jesus fed
over five thousand people with only that
little bit of food.

Just for Fun

Ask the person who makes your lunch to
fix bread and fish for you to eat.
Ask that person to read Jesus' words to
you from Matthew 5.

Now those who had eaten were about
five thousand men, besides women and
children.

Matthew 14:21

It's a Fact

Jesus once walked on the water!

It was a stormy night. Jesus' followers were on their boat fishing. They saw someone walking toward them on top of the water. At first they were afraid. Then they saw it was Jesus. He could walk on water!

Just for Fun

Draw a picture of Jesus walking on the sea. Be sure to make it a stormy sea.

Now in the fourth watch of the night
Jesus went to them, walking on the sea.

Matthew 14:25

It's a Fact

A dead man came back to life!

One day Jesus' enemies killed Him. His friends buried Him in a grave. But after three days, Jesus lived again. Today Jesus lives in heaven.

Just for Fun

Ask an adult to read the Bible story about Jesus' resurrection.

[Jesus] is not here; for He is risen, as He said.

Matthew 28:6

It's a Fact

Jesus once healed a person who could not walk!

Four people had a friend who could not walk. They brought their friend to Jesus. Jesus blessed the man and healed the man so he could walk.

Just for Fun

Thank God for your legs and feet.
Thank Him that you can run and jump.

"Arise, take up your bed, and go to your house."

Mark 2:11

It's a Fact

Jesus once calmed a stormy sea!

Jesus and His followers were on a boat. A terrible storm began. The boat was about to sink. Jesus spoke to the storm. He told the storm to stop. Then the storm stopped, and the sea was quiet.

Just for Fun

Put some water in a sink. Blow on the water gently. See how the wind makes the water move.

Jesus said, "Peace, be still!" And the
wind ceased and there was a great calm.

Mark 4:39

It's a Fact

Jesus helped a blind person to see!

A blind man heard Jesus coming. He called out for Jesus to help him. Jesus said, "What do you want Me to do?" The man said, "I want to see." So, Jesus healed the man and made him able to see!

Just for Fun

You can be like Jesus by helping someone. Think of something nice to do for someone you love and do it.

Then Jesus said to him, "Go your way; your faith has made you well." And immediately he received his sight.

Mark 10:52

It's a Fact

Mary got a message from an angel!

God has some special messengers. They are called *angels*. One angel was named Gabriel. Gabriel came to tell Mary that she was going to have a baby. The baby would be the Son of God. His name would be Jesus.

Just for Fun

Using your crayons and art paper, draw a picture of a beautiful angel. Put the angel in your room. It will remind you that God loves you.

Then the angel said to her, "Do not be afraid, Mary, for you have found favor with God."

Luke 1:30

It's a Fact

God gave special powers!

God's very special servants on earth were called apostles. God helped the apostles to do *miracles*. Making blind people see or the lame to walk is a miracle. Only God can do miracles.

Just for Fun

Pretend that you are one of God's apostles. What wonderful thing would you like for God to help you do?

Now God worked unusual miracles by
the hands of Paul.

Acts 19:11

It's a Fact

There is a war being fought between good and bad!

God is always good. The devil is bad. But God is stronger than the devil. The devil will try to get you to be bad. But God can help you to be good.

Just for Fun

Say a prayer to God. Ask Him to help you be good. Then tell the devil to get away!

You are of God, little children . . . He who is in you is greater than he who is in the world.

1 John 4:4

It's a Fact

God is love and love is God!

Did you know that God and love are the same? So when you show love to someone, you are showing what God is like.

Just for Fun

Think of someone you can show love to. Now make a list of things to do that will show love.

He who does not love does not know
God, for God is love.

1 John 4:8

Additional copies of this book
and other books in this series are available
from your local bookstore.

My Very First Book of Prayers
My Very First Book on God
My Very First Book of Bible Lessons
My Very First Book of Bible Words
My Very First Book of Bible Heroes
My Very First Book of Bible Questions
My Very First Book of God's Animals

If you have enjoyed this book, or if it has
impacted your life, we would like to hear from you.
Please contact us at:

Honor Kidz
Department E
P.O. Box 55388
Tulsa, Oklahoma 74155
Or by e-mail at info@honorbooks.com